D0382344

ADAM VOILAND

ABCs
FROM SPACE

A Discovered Alphabet

A Paula Wiseman Book
SIMON & SCHUSTER BOOKS FOR YOUNG READERS
New York London Toronto Sydney New Delhi

Note to Parents and Teachers

As a science writer for a website called NASA Earth Observatory, I spend lots of time making and writing about pictures that come from satellites flying around Earth. A few years ago, I noticed a cloud of smoke over Canada that had the shape of a *V*.

This got me wondering . . . would it be possible to find the entire alphabet in satellite images of Earth? The answer, it turns out, is yes! After looking at places from Antarctica to the Arctic and everywhere in between, I found enough features that—even if not perfect—had shapes similar to the letters of the alphabet.

Finding all twenty-six letters was a challenge. I probably looked through thousands of pictures before finally narrowing down to what you see in this book. Finding the *R* was especially tough. Nature does not often put diagonal, straight, and curved lines next to one another. For the same reason, *B* was also hard to find. On the other hand, *O*'s and *S*'s were everywhere. Many volcanoes and impact craters make ovals, and lots of meandering rivers make *S*-shapes.

One of the best parts about the search was that I got to learn about some of the most fascinating and beautiful places on our planet. I explored rips in Earth's surface spilling hot lava, clouds swirling around snowy mountains, fires chewing holes in lush forests, glaciers slithering down icy mountain slopes, and much more.

I could not have done this project alone. If my parents had not encouraged me to appreciate the natural world, I doubt I would have had the patience to look through so many satellite images of our planet. If government agencies, including NASA (National Aeronautics and Space Administration), USGS (United States Geological Survey), and NOAA (National Oceanic and Atmospheric Administration) did not build satellites and make data from them publicly available, finding these letters would have been impossible. Jesse Allen, a friend and colleague, helped me with the images. Katherine Mann, my wife, helped me with the text.

I hope you enjoy the book and take care of our beautiful planet!

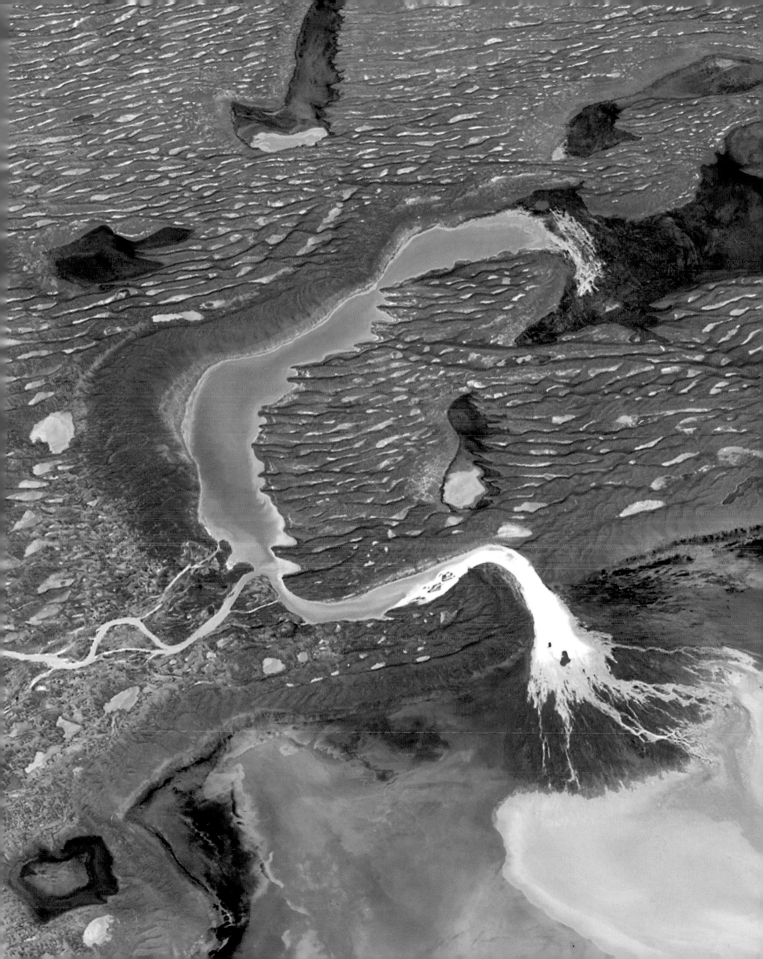

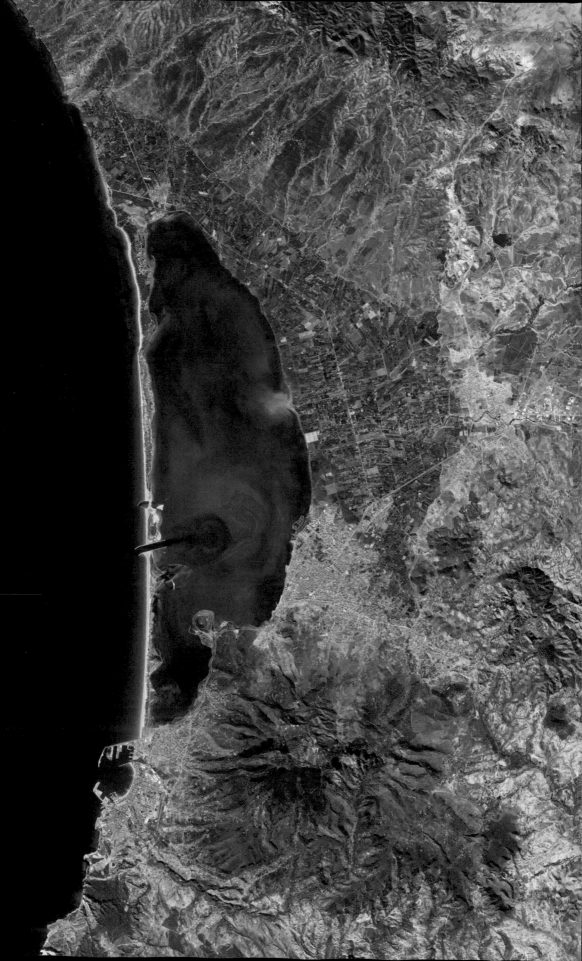

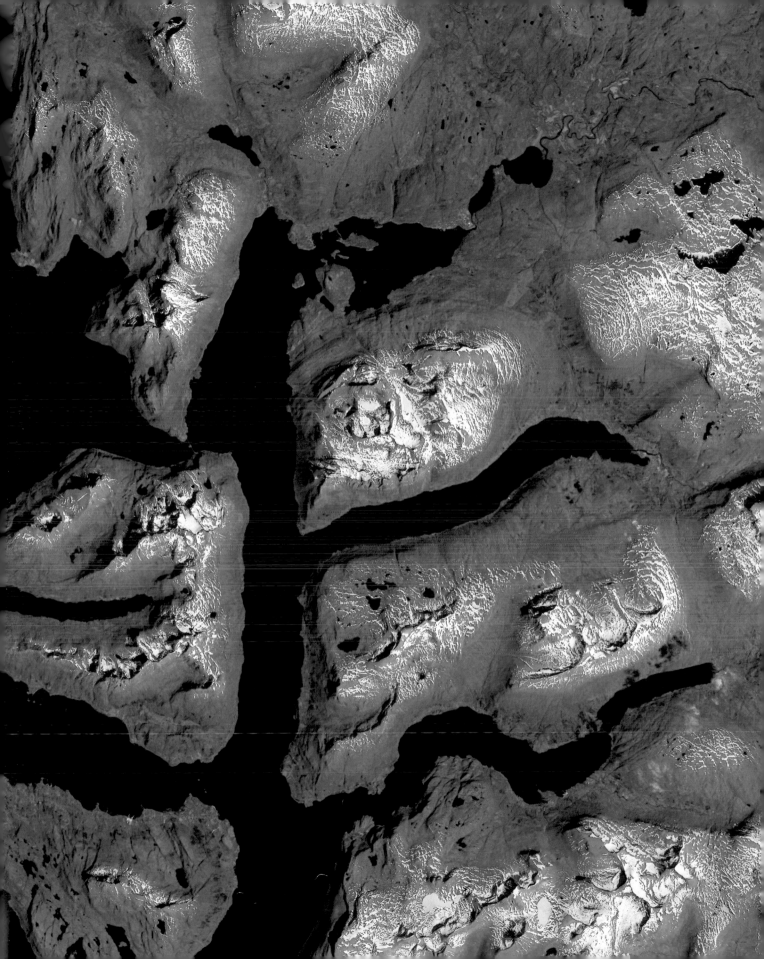

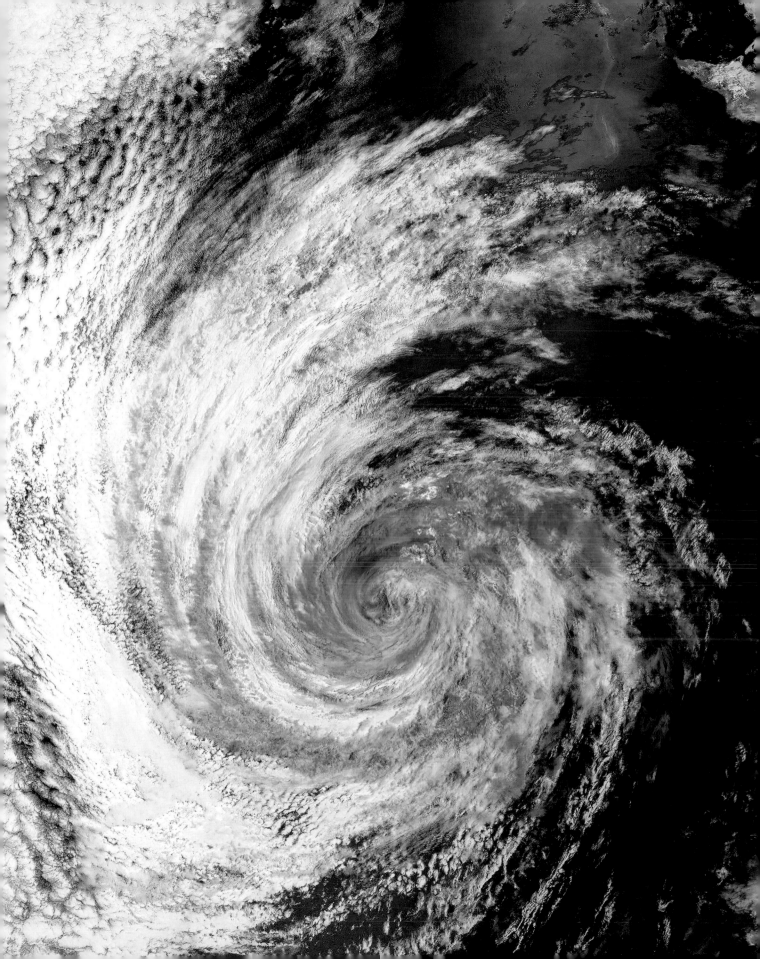

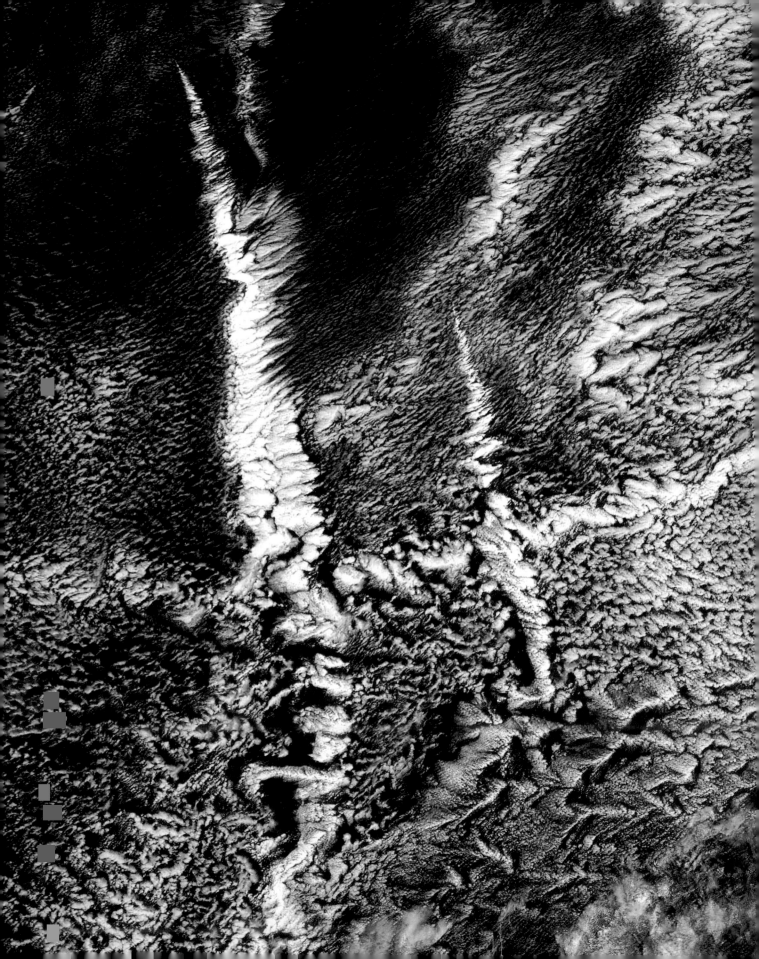

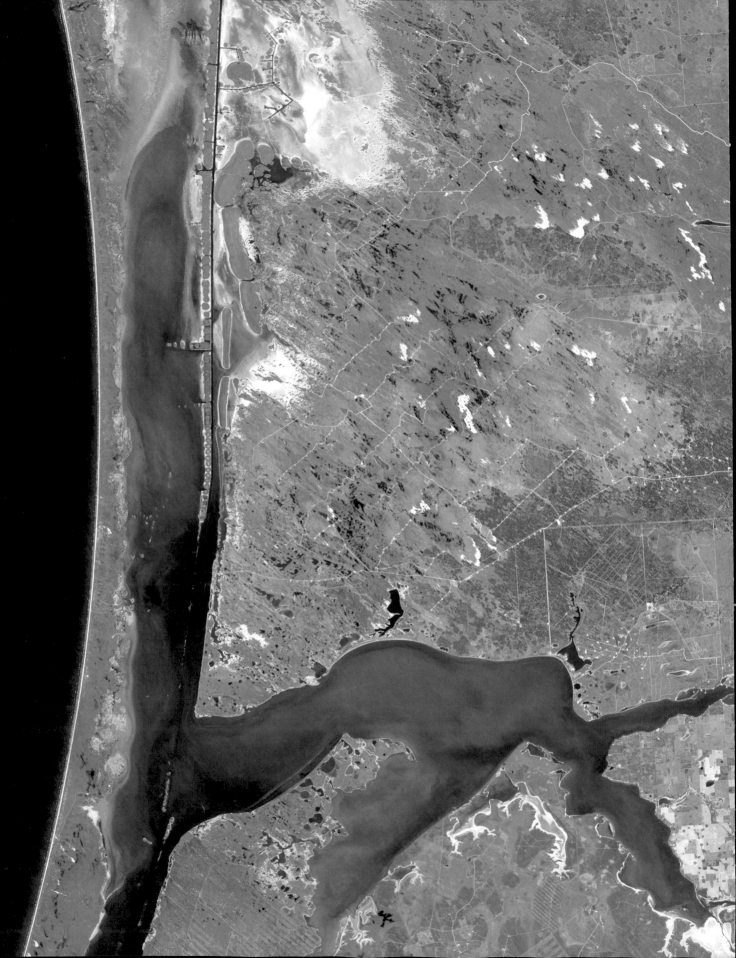

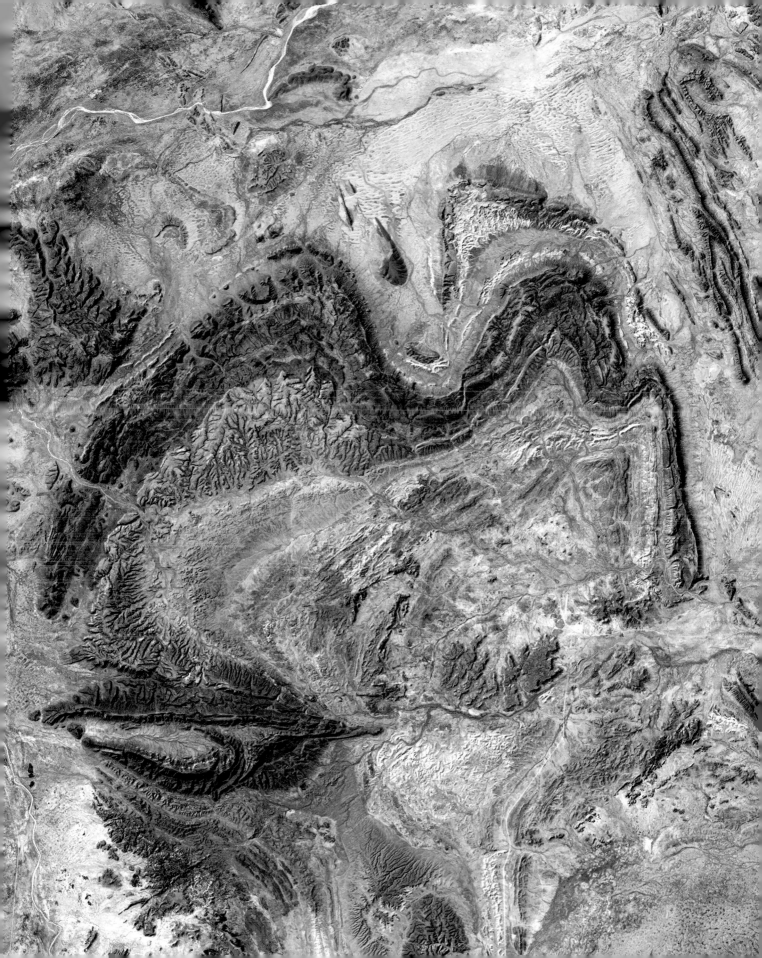

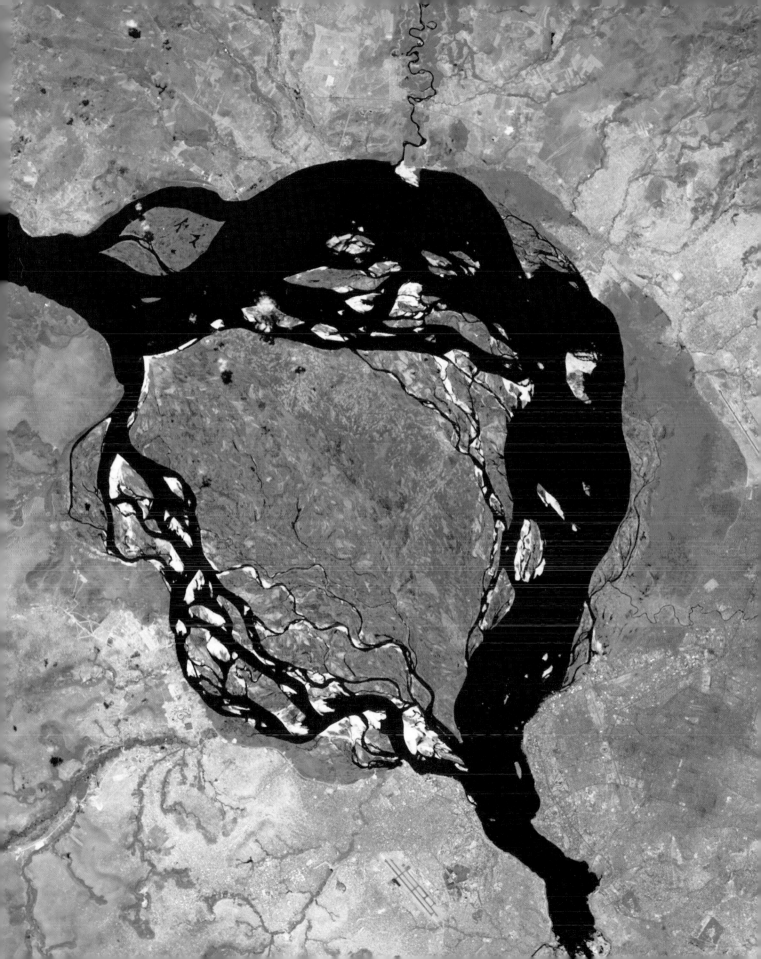

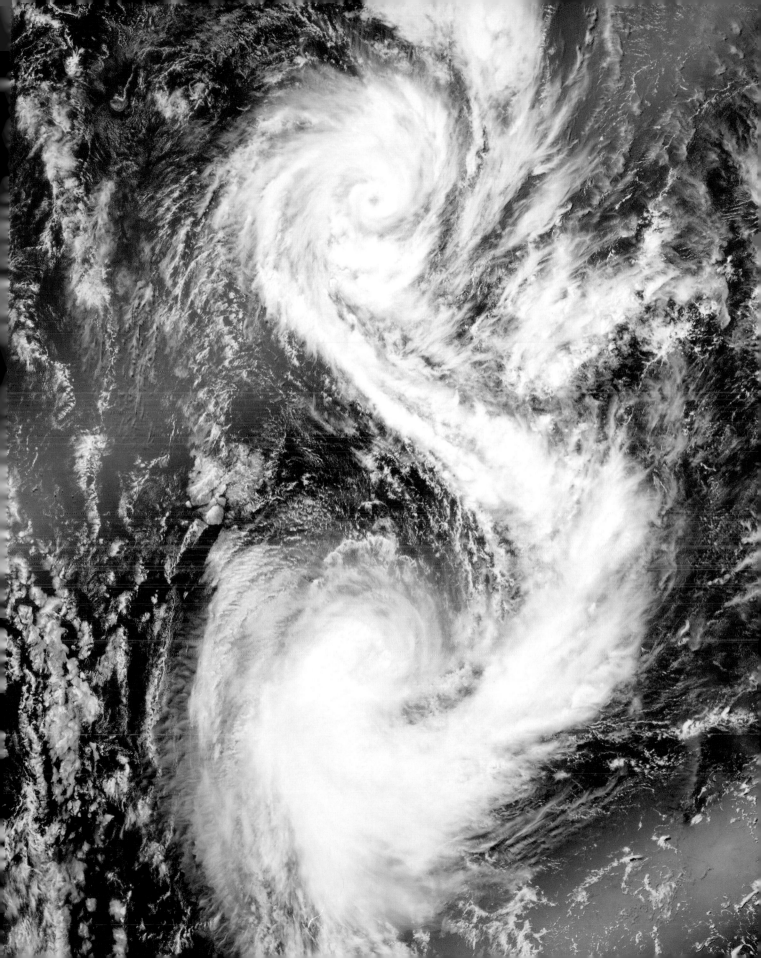

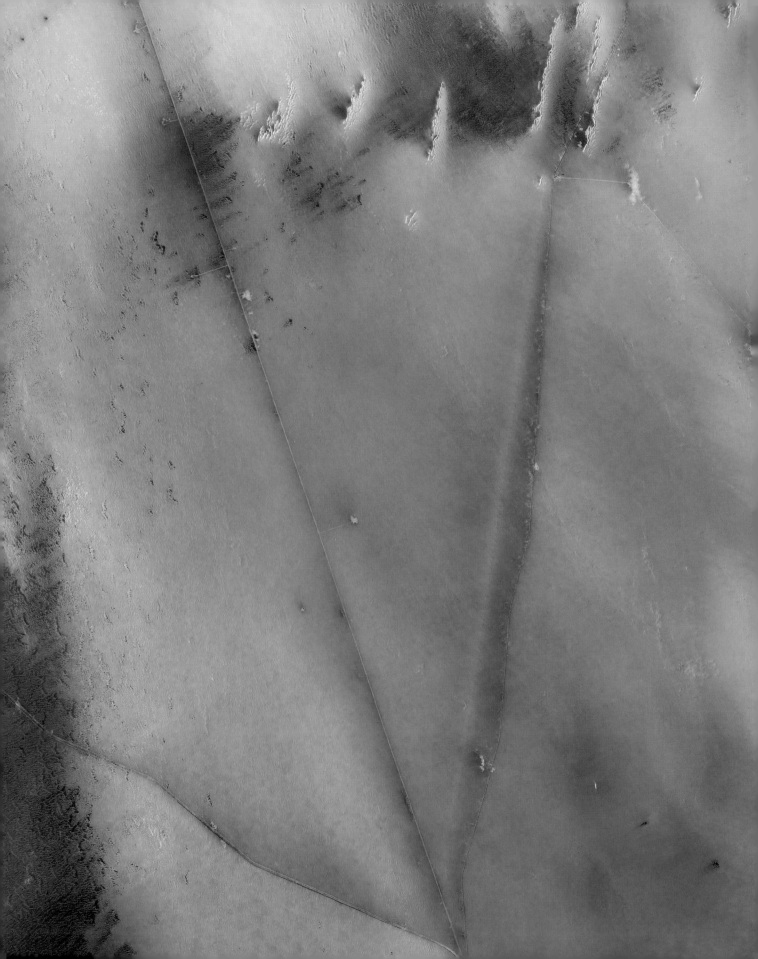

A

Lake Mjøsa in Norway—Farmland and forest (red) topped with a dusting of snow (white) surround Lake Mjøsa—Norway's largest lake—on a spring day. Notice the layer of ice (light blue) in the southernmost part of the lake.

Date: March 21, 2015
Satellite: Landsat 8
Sensor: OLI

Image Type: False-color. Made using measurements of invisible (near-infrared) and visible (red and green) light.

B

Clouds in the South Pacific—Gaps in a sheet of bright clouds reveal the much darker ocean below. The clouds were located near the Tuamotus, a chain of French Polynesian coral atolls in the South Pacific.

Date: March 5, 2016
Satellite: Terra
Sensor: MODIS

Image Type: Natural-color. Made using measurements of visible (red, green, and blue) light.

C

Lake Eyre in Australia—Water (purple) from Kalaweerina Creek drains into part of Lake Eyre, the lowest geographical point on the continent of Australia. Located in South Australia, the lake is usually dry and fills with water only during floods.

Date: February 3, 2015
Satellite: Landsat 8
Sensor: OLI

Image Type: False-color. Made using measurements of invisible (near-infrared) and visible (red and green) light.

D

Marchica Lagoon in Morocco—A thin sandbar separates the shallow Marchica lagoon (turquoise) from the Mediterranean Sea (dark blue). Towns and cities (gray) as well as vegetation (red) surround the lagoon.

Date: February 2, 2016
Sensor: OLI
Satellite: Landsat 8

Image Type: False-color. Made using observations of invisible (shortwave-infrared and near-infrared) and visible (red) light.

E

Fjords in Northern Norway—Several narrow fjords come together in the form of an *E* in this remote part of northern Norway. Between the fjords (blue), there are hills bursting with plant life (green) and capped with snow (white).

Date: July 6, 2014
Satellite: Landsat 8
Sensor: OLI

Image Type: False-color. Made using measurements of invisible (shortwave-infrared) and visible (red) light.

F

Grazing Lands in Australia—Grazing lands (light blue) in the Tambo River Basin in southeastern Victoria appear brighter than the surrounding forests (dark blue) of the Australian Alps. Sheep and cattle are commonly raised in this area.

Date: December 27, 2015
Satellite: Landsat 8
Sensor: OLI

Image type: Natural-color. Made using measurements of visible (blue) and invisible (shortwave-infrared and near-infrared) light.

Tropical Storm Douglas in the Pacific Ocean—Tropical Storm
Douglas churns off the western coast of Mexico. Though the storm did not strike land, it did produce winds of 51 miles per hour before breaking down a few days later. Clouds containing crystals of ice appear orange; clouds composed entirely of liquid water are white.

Date: July 4, 2014
Satellite: Terra
Sensor: MODIS

Image Type: False-color. Made using measurements of visible (blue) and invisible (shortwave-infrared) light.

Ship Tracks Over the Pacific Ocean—Narrow clouds (yellow-white)
caused by ships trail across the Pacific Ocean (black) near Baja California, Mexico. Tiny particles are released into the air as part of a ship's exhaust fumes. Water collects around these particles to form narrow clouds, which are called ship tracks.

Date: June 27, 2013
Satellite: Terra
Sensor: MODIS

Image Type: False-color. Made using measurements of visible (blue) light and invisible (shortwave-infrared) light.

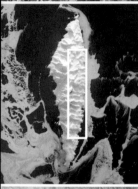

Smith Island off Antarctica—Swirls of drifting sea ice surround Smith
Island (white), an icy island north of the Antarctic Peninsula. Several glaciers, which are rivers of slow-moving ice, spill off the mountainous backbone of the island.

Date: August 26, 2014
Satellite: Landsat 8
Sensor: OLI

Image Type: Natural-color. Made using measurements of visible (red, green, and blue) light.

Lincoln National Forest in New Mexico—Forests (bright green) in
the Smokey Bear Ranger District of Lincoln National Forest stand out amid the surrounding desert landscape (tan). A burn scar (red) is visible in the lower right of the image.

Date: May 6, 2016,
Satellite: Landsat 8
Sensor: OLI

Image Type: False-color. Made using measurements of invisible (short-wave infrared and near-infrared) light and visible (green) light.

Ship Tracks near the Kamchatka Peninsula—Ship track clouds
(yellow-white) cross over the Pacific Ocean (black) east of the Kamchatka Peninsula. Ship track clouds, which form because of ship exhaust, tend to be brighter and last longer than other clouds that form naturally.

Date: April 29, 2013
Satellite: Terra
Sensor: MODIS

Image Type: False-color. Made using measurements of visible (blue) and invisible (shortwave-infrared) light.

Laguna Madre in Texas—Padre Island separates the waters of a shallow lagoon named Laguna Madre (light blue) from the Gulf of Mexico (dark blue). The lagoon averages a depth of just 3.6 feet.

Date: May 6, 2016,
Satellite: Landsat 8
Sensor: OLI

Image Type: False-color. Made using observations of invisible (shortwave-infrared) and visible (red) light.

Rock Formations in Australia—A curving ridge of rock in Northern Territory sweeps across the desert landscape. The mountains in this area formed millions of years ago, when the shifting of Earth's surface transformed the flat sea floor into rugged mountains.

Date: March 30, 2016
Satellite: Landsat 8
Sensor: OLI

Image Type: False-color. Made using observations of invisible (shortwave-infrared and near-infrared) and visible (red) light.

Clouds off the Coast of Western Sahara—Parallel lines of clouds drift over the Atlantic Ocean off the coast of Western Sahara. Oceans tend to be pretty cloudy places; roughly 67 percent of the sky over oceans is cloudy.

Date: April 23, 2016
Satellite: Landsat 8
Sensor: OLI

Image Type: False-color. Made using measurements of visible (green and red) and invisible (shortwave-infrared) light.

Richat Structure in Mauritania—This circular feature was once thought to be an impact crater or a volcano, but geologists now think that the structure formed because of the power of windblown sand and flowing water. The wind has uncovered alternating layers of folded rock (purple, green, red, tan) in the shape of a bull's-eye.

Date: May 20, 2016
Satellite: Landsat 8
Sensor: OLI

Image type: False-color. Made using measurements of invisible (shortwave-infrared and near-infrared) and visible (green) light.

Euphrates River in Syria—The Euphrates River (blue) winds past Raqqa, Syria, (gray) as the river flows southeast toward Iraq and the Persian Gulf. Farm fields (red) are located near the river as well as along a loop formed by an irrigation canal.

Date: August 29, 2015
Satellite: Landsat 8
Sensor: OLI

Image Type: False-color. Made using measurements of invisible (near-infrared) and visible (red and green) light.

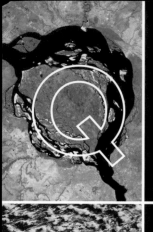

Malebo Pool in the Congo—The Congo River widens as it makes its way around Bamu Island along the border of the Republic of the Congo and the Democratic Republic of the Congo. The capital cities of these two countries—Brazzaville and Kinshasa—are located on opposites sides of the river. The cities (gray) are surrounded by tropical forests (green) and farmland (yellow).

Date: July 28, 2013
Satellite: Landsat 8
Sensor: OLI

Image Type: False-color. Made using measurements of invisible (shortwave-infrared) and visible (red) light.

Clouds in the Southern Ocean—A swirl in a cloud formation (blue) appears in a turbulent area over the Southern Ocean (black). Strong winds and storms are common around Antarctica in July, which is the middle of winter in the Southern Hemisphere.

Date: July 20, 2016
Satellite: Terra
Sensor: MODIS

Image Type: False-color. Made using observations of invisible (infrared) and visible (red) light.

Twin Storms in the Indian Ocean—Twin tropical cyclones—named Eunice and Diamondra—churn over the central Indian Ocean. While neither storm was particularly strong, how close they were to each other was unusual.

Date: January 28, 2015
Satellite: Suomi NPP
Sensor: VIIRS

Image Type: Natural-color. Made using measurements of visible (red, green, and blue) light.

Moulouya River in Morocco—The Moulouya River and one of its smaller tributary streams intersect in northern Morocco near the town of Oujda. Lots of farmland (dark blue) is present along the river.

Date: April 22, 2016.
Satellite: Landsat 8
Sensor: OLI

Image Type: False-color. Made using measurements of visible (blue) and invisible light (short-wave infrared).

Two Rivers in the Republic of the Congo—The low-lying Lefini and Nambouli Rivers meet within a wildlife reserve in the Republic of the Congo. The two rivers have carved deep valleys into the surrounding plateau. Dense forests (dark green) are clustered within the valleys along the rivers. Grasslands (light green) cover the plateaus.

Date: August 13, 2013
Satellite: Landsat 8
Sensor: OLI

Image Type: False-color. Made using measurements of invisible (shortwave-infrared) and visible (red light).

Water Pipeline and Road in Libya—A large water pipeline and highway come together to form a V-shape in a desolate part of the Sahara Desert in southeastern Libya. The pipeline is part of the Great Man-Made River, a huge project designed to transport water from beneath the desert in the interior of Libya to cities along the coast.

Date: March 13, 2016
Satellite: Landsat 8
Sensor: OLI

Image Type: False-color. Made using measurements of invisible (shortwave-infrared) and visible (green and blue) light.

Sea Ice in the Arctic Ocean—On a spring day, cracks have formed in sea ice floating in the Arctic Ocean west of Axel Heiberg Island, which is part of Canada. Winds or ocean currents usually cause cracks like this to open up.

Date: April 26, 2015
Satellite: Landsat 8
Sensor: OLI

Image Type: Natural-color. Made using observations of visible (red, green, blue) light.

Fjords in Southern Norway—Two fjords filled with seawater from the North Sea intersect at a sharp angle. Look for valleys dotted with farmland (light green) and small villages (gray) contrasting with forests (dark green) flanking ridges that have been sculpted by glaciers.

Date: September 15, 2014
Satellite: Landsat 8
Sensor: OLI

Image Type: False-color. Made using observations of invisible (shortwave-infrared) and visible (red) light.

Two Rivers in Iraq—Where the Tigris and Great Zab Rivers converge in northern Iraq, lush farmland (green) along the banks of the rivers (blue) offers a stark contrast to the surrounding desert (tan). Mosul, one of Iraq's largest cities, appears as a gray area along the river in the upper left.

Date: November 3, 2015
Satellite: Landsat 8
Sensor: OLI

Image Type: False-color. Made using observations of invisible (shortwave-infrared, near-infrared) and visible (red) light.

Snow in the United States—A slow-moving winter storm dropped a zigzagging band of snow (blue) that cuts through parts of Colorado, Kansas, Oklahoma, New Mexico, and Texas. In some areas, more than three feet of snow fell.

Date: November 26, 2013
Satellite: Aqua
Sensor: MODIS

Image Type: False-color. Made using observations of invisible (infrared) and visible (red) light.

Map of Letter Locations

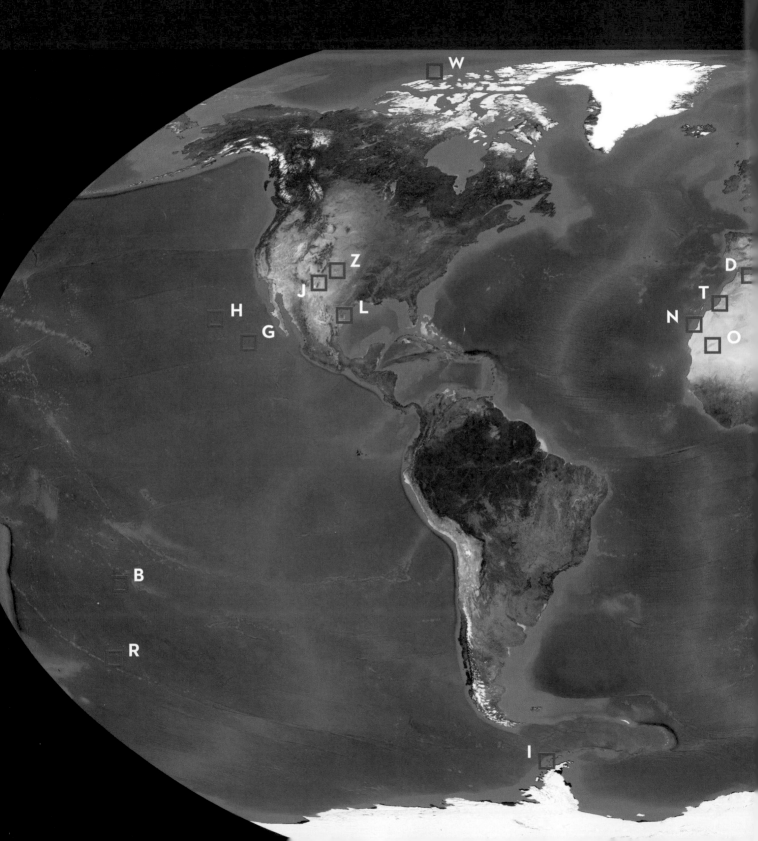

The clouds, rock formations, and other features highlighted in this book are scattered around the world on multiple continents and oceans. This was not by design. For each individual letter, I focused my search on areas that I thought would have land features or weather that was likely to feature a particular shape. For instance, I knew that places with fjords, glaciers, and sea ice would form the straight lines needed for letters like A, X, E, and W. Likewise, I knew that ocean clouds were a good source of the curves needed in letters like B, G, R, and S.

Map by Jesse Allen, using data from MODIS and GEBCO.

FAQs—Images

Are these photographs taken by astronauts?

No, these images were collected by robotic satellites—Landsat 8, Terra, Aqua, or Suomi NPP. Satellites are machines that fly around Earth taking measurements of our planet. Landsat 8, which collected most of the images in this book, flies 438 miles above the surface, about the distance between Boston and Washington, DC. The satellite weighs about 3,300 pounds, roughly the weight of a small car.

What is the difference between a satellite image and a photograph?

Photographs are made when *visible* light reflects off objects and is recorded by cameras on either film or digital film. Satellites, on the other hand, can see types of light that are *invisible* to human eyes as well as visible light. Satellites have sensors similar to cameras on board that can measure this invisible light.

What is a "natural-color" satellite image?

All the pictures you see in this book are made by satellites measuring how much visible or invisible light is bouncing off parts of Earth, such as clouds in the sky or forests on the ground. Scientists can make "natural-color" images that look similar to what human eyes would see if they were looking down on Earth from space. Natural-color images are made with measurements of visible light, not invisible light. A few important types of visible light are red, green, and blue light.

What is a "false-color" satellite image?

False-color satellite pictures combine satellite measurements of invisible light and visible light—making the invisible visible to us! Familiar things on Earth can have a very unexpected look in false-color. Forests that appear green to our eyes can be red or blue in false-color. White clouds can look orange or black. Important types of invisible light that are used to make the false-color images in this book are near-infrared and shortwave-infrared light.

How are false-color satellite images useful?

One of the handy things about false-color pictures is that they allow us to see details that would usually be invisible, even if you happened to be an astronaut looking down on Earth from outer space. As a result, false-color pictures are very useful for meteorologists forecasting the weather, miners figuring out where to dig, and for firefighters monitoring a forest fire.

Do all four satellites see the same amount of detail?

No, some satellites see more detail than others. Landsat 8 has a sensor called OLI (Operational Land Imager) that sees enough detail to make out individual buildings. Terra and Aqua have a sensor called MODIS (Moderate Resolution Imaging Spectroradiometer) that sees a much wider area. MODIS is good at observing large features like hurricanes; OLI is good at observing smaller features like roads or streams.

FAQs—Science

How do clouds form?

Clouds are made of drops of water or ice crystals floating in the sky. Clouds form when invisible bits of water in a gaseous state rise and cool down. As the bits of water cool, they begin to stick to tiny pieces of dust, salt, or other particles in the sky, creating cloud droplets. Over time, the cloud droplets grow bigger and bigger until they eventually become raindrops that tumble back to Earth's surface. See the letters B, G, H, K, N, R, and S for examples of clouds.

What causes layers of rock to bend?

Rock layers can bend for several reasons, but one of the most important has to do with the shifting of the giant, rigid plates that make up Earth's surface. When these plates run against one another or directly collide, they can fold, twist, and warp rock layers as if the rock were taffy. This process creates mountain ranges. See the letters M and O for examples of bending rock layers.

What causes sea ice to crack?

In the frigid, dark winters in the Arctic and Antarctica, a layer of ice forms on the surface of the ocean. As temperatures warm in the spring, the ice breaks into smaller pieces and eventually melts away. But even in the height of winter, winds or currents can cause cracks in the ice. See the I and W images for examples of sea ice.

What makes rivers meander?

Rivers rarely flow in straight lines. Rather they bend back and forth in curved shapes called meanders. Usually these meanders get started because a minor obstruction—say a few rocks or a log—partially block the flow of a stream. As the water flows around the obstacle, it begins to carve away more land on one side of the river than the other. At the same time, the river drops mud and sand on the opposite side. Over time, the curve gets sharper. See the C, P, Q, and Y images for examples of meandering streams and rivers.

How to fjords form?

Fjords are long, narrow, water-filled valleys that usually have steep cliffs on either side. The presence of a fjord is a clue that massive pieces of ice, called glaciers, flowed over and sculpted the landscape in the past. Glaciers are so massive that they can grind away rock to make deep valleys. If sea levels rise and the bottoms of these valleys flood, fjords will form. See the letters A, E, and X for examples of fjords.

Aqua: an Earth-observing satellite launched by NASA in 2002

atoll: a ring of coral around a shallow body of water called a lagoon

burn scar: charred vegetation left behind after a fire

desert: a dry area with little green vegetation

fjord: a narrow inlet of the sea between high cliffs

farmland: land used to grow crops or raise animals for food

forest: a large area covered by trees and shrubs

glacier: a mass of slow-moving ice on land

geologists: scientists who study processes that affect Earth's land, water, and rocks

impact crater: a hole in the ground caused by material from space crashing into Earth

infrared light: an invisible type of light that has longer wavelengths than visible light; near-infrared light and shortwave-infrared light are types of infrared light that are widely used by scientists to study Earth

irrigation canal: a waterway designed to bring water closer to crops

lagoon: a shallow body of water separated from a larger body of water by a barrier

Landsat 8: an Earth-observing satellite launched in 2013 by NASA and the US Geological Survey.

Moderate Resolution Imaging Spectroradiometer (MODIS): a key sensor on the Terra and Aqua satellites that measures invisible and visible types of light

Operational Land Imager (OLI): a satellite sensor on Landsat 8 that observes both visible and invisible types of light

particles: a small bit of something

plateau: an area of relatively high and flat ground

sea ice: frozen ocean water

ship exhaust: waste gases or air expelled from a ship engine

ship tracks: linear clouds that form around particles of dust and other substances in the air; the particles come from the fumes of ship exhaust

Southern Hemisphere: the southern half of Earth

Suomi NPP: an Earth-observing satellite launched in 2011 by several US government agencies

Terra: an Earth-observing satellite launched by NASA in 1999

Visible Infrared Imaging Radiometer Suite (VIIRS): a satellite sensor on Suomi NPP that observes both visible and invisible types of light

vegetation: all the plant life in an area

visible light: light that is visible to the human eye

volcano: a break in Earth's surface that occasionally vents hot gases and liquid rock

For Mae

Want to Learn More?

Learn more about false-color satellite images:
http://earthobservatory.nasa.gov/Features/FalseColor/

Learn more about the electromagnetic spectrum and invisible types of light:
https://science.nasa.gov/ems

Learn more about how to interpret natural-color satellite images:
http://earthobservatory.nasa.gov/Features/ColorImage/

SIMON & SCHUSTER BOOKS FOR YOUNG READERS
An imprint of Simon & Schuster Children's Publishing Division
1230 Avenue of the Americas, New York, New York 10020
Copyright © 2017 by Adam Voiland
All rights reserved, including the right of reproduction in whole or in part in any form.
SIMON & SCHUSTER BOOKS FOR YOUNG READERS is a trademark of Simon & Schuster, Inc.
For information about special discounts for bulk purchases, please contact Simon & Schuster Special Sales at 1-866-506-1949 or business@simonandschuster.com.
The Simon & Schuster Speakers Bureau can bring authors to your live event. For more information or to book an event, contact the Simon & Schuster Speakers Bureau at 1-866-248-3049 or visit our website at www.simonspeakers.com.
Book design by Krista Vossen
The text for this book was set in Geometric Slab 712.
The illustrations for this book were rendered in Adobe Photoshop.
Image data was downloaded from the U.S. Geological Survey's Earth Explorer (http://earthexplorer.usgs.gov),
Snapsat (http://snapsat.org), or NASA's LANCE/EOSDIS Rapid Response
(https://earthdata.nasa.gov/earth-observation-data/near-real-time/rapid-response)
Manufactured in China
0617 SCP
First Edition
2 4 6 8 10 9 7 5 3 1
CIP data for this book is available from the Library of Congress.
ISBN 978-1-4814-9428-1
ISBN 978-1-4814-9429-8 (eBook)